Now
Time

Mattie McClane
Myrtle Hedge Press

Now Time

To my mother

Contents

Now Time

The clouds build
toward the lilies;
the sky is faintly purple
with rain. These words lend hope
or a consolation from being away.
The trees are still as if they are listening
to mild rumblings; thunder
begins in the distance and comes closer to home.
One wonders what happens now, the old computer
was so hacked. so undone, that another
replaces it. My soul, my soul longs for beauty
and to be concise in all things.

I think of things unresolved, of loose ends
and unfinished questions. Of course, when
we are young we believe that we can walk
away from turmoil. But it finds us like work,
like the carpet that needs sweeping
or the grass that grows long. It has found me.

And I do long for the pleasant past when
worries were passed over. I do long for when
I was able to express deepest thoughts without
anxiety. I think I've been wrong for sounding
so right, for saying what nobody can know
for sure. Be wary of quick inspiration and easy-flowing words.
Words come hard when they are yours. I say we push
on moisture-swollen doors, an immovable thought;
but I can break through and the words will look like
they belong in rich hotels with foil wrapped candy
on pillows. They'll be as sweet as wedding icing
or summer clover. You pick. I can pick through
words until the exhausted verb falls on the page, a swoon
like movie lovers with thick lips and strange names.
Only I will find it hard to be fake; I will find it
difficult to frame silly ideas in the noblest terms. Go figure,
a model's shape, rectangles, squares and oblong boobs.
I am the fool today because I thought I could know
truth and it ran out the opened gate or under, yes under
the fence when I wasn't looking or was reading
the New York Times, the only newspaper that can use
the word, sublime, how excellent, how perfect, just elevated
like a spike heel, I will want to be healed
because I didn't really know a damned thing
with my multiple degrees.

A person should have one degree, preferably in chemistry
and know the facts, measurements, atomic numbers, even
naturally occurring elements. Leave it to no one to judge,
to surmise motives; it'll turn one
into a toady and then what?
One will carry a footstool with a satin covering messed up
with boot black. Remember the accusation that one didn't
know shit from shoe shine? That's how it happens, any toady
might tell me. Let's move on though... Words won't slide
on a page; they're not zealous baseball players or skaters.
I tell you they resist and would laugh at me maybe if they
could tell what I'm trying to do.

Newspapers are full of words, and they go out everyday.
They can't hang around saying the same thing like books.
Who can throw out a book?
Probably a sinister man or an anal woman
who keeps her magazines
on a coffee table. Books are for keeps. That is the unspoken
vow and it is real, all those words on parade, floats at a
county fair celebration,
one after another, but nobody throws candy and nobody
waves from convertibles. Books are stately, no Nebraska
irrigation machine ever
looked so fine, a lofty and noticeable presence.

Words aren't easy and books do not go to recyclers,
they offer no choices of plastic;
it's paper all the way. Someone said it was an apple
that caused the problem
but it was paper.

It's hot today-h-o-t-t, as the man at the farmer's market says.
He sold me a
paper sack of grass seed. Seed is as pretty as oats. I threw
the seed with a hand-
spreader and dogs trampled any beginnings. They did not
know it was
for the lawn. It was a tickertape parade or a confetti
extravaganza. The dogs
thought a war was over.

Unresolved matters are everywhere, the war in Iraq. Nobody
knows why we're there, oil, freedom, we're the liberators
of people
who didn't want to be free, we're unwanted helping hands,
setting up democracy in a tradition of tyranny. Tyrants
wear mustaches
and the media reports on their snacking habits, no
potato chips
for a menace. The media doesn't report harsh words
about America,

because they are the bad guys. We are good, have usually
been good in history.

I turned on the porch light last night,
wanted everyone to know
that there's a house in the woods. The bugs swooned around
the light; light is tequila to them; they are intoxicated
by the light.
No deliveryman came, no UPS, no Fed Ex,
no courier of any kind,
so someone flipped the switch, and it was trees in darkness,
trees see nothing, and they don't use words.
Trees are poems, aren't pretenders
or rhetoricians. They could care less about the political
implications
in narratives.

Pink myrtle blooms in September, late
like news about a job
when one wants to work
at a desk, a sturdy table
to spread out papers
meant for file cabinets
ancient orange, painted
for home offices, and the buds
have yellow seeds, we're back

to seeds that make everything grow
and prosper; it is a prosperous era,
a deep-pocket time, jingle coins silver
but there is no gold in plastic
just a monthly statement
when the myrtles bloom late
like expecting a baby; one
go to the doctor and say
the water has broken, water, drip,
up to ceilings in places after
a record number of hurricanes,
who will say to generations
that Chicago is the Windy City,
New Orleans knows better
under the events center thousands
take shelter.

The disaster was worse than expected
with hundreds missing, hundreds dead.
Rehnquist dies and now the battle
is for the Supreme Court
and the catastrophe is nearly forgotten
to politics. "Today" is the strongest word
there isn't another like it with so much agency,
so much urgency, and promises kept.
If I can do it today, I'm a healer,

a triumph, a success story, the world marvels
at heroism. Where are the heroes? Did they die
in the early to mid 20th century? Are they
gone? The air is clear
as if it were a sandwich bag;
it is clear and keeps fresh, pears hanging
from a bowed-over tree
with a hundred limbs aimed
toward the ground, dusty ground,
and one looks for rain
but the forecaster says sunny
more dryness, more uncertainty.
Yet, perhaps hope is in the falling mercury,
down it goes for the ninth month, changing green
to multi-colored horizons,
one tires of the monotony of illness
to too much heat, too much stillness,
and longs for newness.
What is new in your bag of tricks?
What thing, gizmo or gadget can win
the popular sentiment
like the dream of affectionate strangers
with kin-like hugs and well-wishes
and longtime curious readers call
or write in wanting
to know where I've been, away

on vacation, always away on vacation
when a call comes from Ohio;
the lady phones from a white barn
with oat bins and calves,
an advertisement painted
on the sliding shed door
so it can be seen from the interstate
by tourists or people going home
to somewhere, a white farmhouse surrounded
by churches and noticeable steeples,
held high from the summer's turning wind
and Dorothy runs for the cellar this time
and no one makes a movie
about her adventures, no one should tell
that story again for another year,
the children do not gather
like they used to in front
of the television and stay up late
to know the fate of the man behind
the curtain; the call will come
in from Eastern Kentucky
and the incoming voice will offer
me everything, every kind of work,
every type of class, and amazement
has her day and will be female
for the purpose of this poem, beware

of the everything offer with little
or no teaching experience.
But one can relax because it pays
nothing, buy a hardcover book
with the proceeds, call oneself
a professional or a very educated person
with a lifelong hobby.

I told the man if I don't know I
will find out become an expert. Everyone loves
an expert, egghead not yet cracked
with indifference. Try to make people care
a little. But they are busy cutting their lawns
and nobody should bother them or maybe
the strangers are fellow church members, cars parked
in the grass, telling of a full house. The lottery bill
passed in North Carolina; they took a chance,
they bet on education funds and a guy
becomes broke wanting to be rich, rich
is it, it doesn't buy groceries, the money buys boats
and ambassadorships in record numbers, part
with rich money today.

If I don't know, I'll become an expert,
a bit overboard. It would be easier, community-like
to say "I don't know" and leave it at that;

that is the smarter thing to do
because you've left the teapot
on and are driving fifty miles per hour
down a city street
and lawyers are sending letters
to inquire
about the last ticket,
rolling through a stop sign
and leaving it upright
for the next person
to abide. So the teapot whistles
and I don't know anything
but Social Security Numbers
and bits from the past, flying
by like wind-driven stiff leaves
in autumn. It isn't okay
to be driven; I thought
it was for a brief time in youth
and then I needed to play catch up
for a long time, and it caught me finally
and I poured two cups of tea
and still drive very fast
because I like power on wheels, a V-6
with brakes all around. I've said it now
with the power of psychotherapy, discuss
your mother and your father

whoever else impressed childhood desire
of ponies and mini-bikes
of green bicycles
with shifters and passing time
with worms
before the rain, when a drop sent water circles
on the pond's surface.

I wait for rain and my menstrual period
both offering relief. I think
about words and loss
about how one can't make a profession
out of them by living them. It's fallacy,
a big mistake to think people ever mean
anything they say or would build temples
if words had power. Lawyers live
on words and blame comes their way,
too flimsy for foundations
too misunderstood to be credible.
A neighbor mows
the grass today; the grass is crunchy, the color
of a wheat field in sweet potato country,
the sweet potato is king here or is tobacco
the amber crowned wonder? I vote
for the wild flowers along the roadside
when the car is moving very fast

and the vision is fleeting, not confined
to elementary encyclopedias
from the 1960s. I wonder about
where things go before they're shut
in a white barn in Ohio. I wonder
if one can cry for not knowing
all that is lost, lost like a diamond
out of its prongs and panic strikes
but nobody cries over a fancy rock
laughable on the carpet assured
of eventual rescue, the dog knocks
it with a paw or the vacuum cleaners comes
so close.

I wonder where things go when they're not quite
gone, the lady with the special shoes
and bad thyroid talked about grieving
about crying in her office. Cry
about an illness and pray
and one knows ones already prayed
much about forgetting
and going on in that V-6
driving, wanting to drive
and to pray in hurricane season. I told
my friend to pray for the people in New Orleans,
and the water came, but it was storm surge

and not the blessing I ask for
when the water nourishes and brings life.

Today, I remember youth
and how nothing
seemed better
than dreams, better
than ability,
and somebody crooned
in an ear, a whisper
and I could do it my way,
one could make every colossal mistake,
overlook what bored
and sometimes
I could be haughty, the snob on call,
because dreams were brilliant
and I was smart, nothing better
to be.

"Smart" falters and still wonders
where these things go
when they're half gone
like the half glass of milk
after thick frosted cinnamon
rolls and you contemplate leaving
the rest or dumping it down

the sink when the guilt
of wasting food enters your mind.
Where do things go
when a trip is half over
and ones on ones way back
having seen tourists' sights
before, the museums,
the grown-over battlefields,
and restored celebrity homes
where the wife raised champion goats
and bragged that they had two udders
and produced warm buckets of milk
like in that Ohio barn
where calves have cream-colored
shag rug faces and well water comes
from a T-like spigot
in the farm's yard? I suppose
that spirited chickens, red chickens
or roosters run into the gravel lane
in front of heavy machinery
painted John Deere green
or International Harvester red
and the shops are nearly gone
where my grandfather cast tools
and made parts for 20 years
or most of a man's lifetime,

was nearly gone, half gone,
but such a man can go fishing
in travel trailers
to Canadian cool waters, large lakes
with loons and red and white lures
and white bent birch trees
where the bark pulls away like paper,
leaves blow like string mops
in the wind, half a wind going
somewhere, wherever things go
when kisses are far and few between
when every sweet word is asked
for and love is half, half love,
like a half note, has its own kind
of beat, and one can dance
however one wants under the moonlight
and I can concisely prepare
speeches and clever remarks
in case a stray listener is found
behind counters at the drug store
or feed store or hardware store. Imagine
the world, and it's full of listeners,
nobody talking, nobody being artful,
everyone has an ear to the garden row
and it smells in front of the white
Ohio farm buildings, the ground is dusty

and no rain will touch it, no rain can fall
today.

It does sprinkle, not buckets
finally wetting hanging leaves
and giving them pure courage
after WWII heroes are gone
and people can say they love,
promise forever
when the mood strikes
them and when the rain falls
the moon is full, going
away from the table, very fast.
It is not a dollar moon
or a dinner plate moon
or a globe cut out of paper
it is a moon with no comparison
and it shines after thunder surprised
the neighborhood, and folks rush
out to mowers and blowers
every engine howls
clippings will be sidelined
and everyone engages in lawn care.
I say it is a blessing when the moon
can only be described as a moon
and a white shed in Illinois protects

canisters of walnuts and wood handled hammers.
At the porch step a woman stands in a housedress
and warns us about the strawberries,
Don't step on them, let no shoes
come near but do crack
the nut with the heavy tool
and remember candy in deep pockets
of old men who loved children
and scare great grandchildren
with their wrinkles and soapy smell. Eat
mashed potatoes and listen to the mantle clock
the world is timeless and sleepy and bored
with so much adult talk. No room
is left unexplored, pictures of favorites
silver combs and stained glass, water from a pump
in the kitchen and the flooring is yellowed
and coals would burn hot if it were winter
in Illinois or Ohio where cars drive fast
and white-faced cows climb up a hill
from the creek. It is a blessing,
this rain opening memory
and taps the skylight when the house
is empty. It is gone now; I tried
to put it on paper and it resisted.
Do your words glide, do they skip,
are they easy on paper, do they tell me

anything I didn't know? It is okay to know
nothing. It is okay to push open that door
and make words sound against the frame.

Ohio

Are you smart, smartest now
and do your dreams
hit wooden porch planks and greet
me kindly like another scene
when mingling strangers
call and invite me
to churches or movies
or to sit in their living rooms?
Say I want nothing but words
and cars that go fast.
Say one is finally smart
enough to give up
every book, every common
quotation, every hint,
every clue. Indians
wait for rain in storybooks;
they dance, are festive.
Crops wait for rain. And the sea
is indifferent. The rain came and now
it has left. I'll wonder where things go
when they are half gone. I'll wonder.

ONE will make paper walls
and tear down wallpaper
The room will be white
like faces in barns and on steep hills
and beside rivers. The myrtle was late
in September and color stays
in one's mind, one's open mind, flooding
with images and people
from some other place.

Rain covers the street tonight
and yet it hesitates to fall
in large drops, drops that pound
against the windows and keep
one awake at night. The walker
does his round with an umbrella,
maybe a golf accessory
because of its blue and white stripes.
Earn your stripes and expect
a glorious heroes' welcome
for brawny carpenters working
in the aftermath of Katrina
or Rita. Ophelia left town before
too many talked about her;
she didn't have the force
to make the evening news,

too little destruction, blown-over
houses are newsworthy,
like the enlisted woman
from West Virginia who wanted
a college education and ended
up on trial for prisoner
abuse in Iraq, today
they arrested a fallen soldier's mother
for sitting close to the White House.
Crawford, Texas was her first camp,
her protest; she wanted someone to listen.
Imagine the world full of listeners,
broadcasters silent, lending
an ear to every hard luck story.
O'Connor says that "charity
is hard and endures." Watch out
for remarkable quotes
and people who love wisdom;
they make no money
and are in the same cell
with Martha Stewart
and the mother who went political
at menopause. Today, scores
sit by televisions and say
she got exactly what she deserved
for expecting justice or for driving

fast to a not-quite Southern city
on the Potomac where somebody
crossed on a black clear night
or were there buckets of rain,
like a message to the other side,
a great leader is coming, great leaders
come and go in monument city
and well-dressed men dine
in expensive restaurants
because somebody else is picking up
the stapled tab, tabulation,
the tabulation is about a score
and winners are chosen daily
like a sweepstakes, like a prom queen
in the crocus tulip daffodil springtime
when the cherry blossoms
unfold in the capital city
before knowledgeable eyes? Never want
to know too much. Plead ignorance,
the Fifth, and don't ask me
to explain the Bill of Rights
or the Constitution
of brave men driving armored tanks;
the tank takes care of numerous concerns
and they will, I'll write home
for answers and instructions

for self-absorbed insights
about how I first began, how peace
ends and how silly men are elected
for four more years. Of course, I know
nothing.

Mt. Evans' hairpin winding curves
going up to the summit
and one can stand straight
at a slick paved lookout
and see no wandering buffalo,
maybe a few white goats
that nobody wants
in a windswept farmyard;
the barn is not open
this time of year
and thoughtless cows stand
in syrup brown grassy fields
and one might feel mountain air
from a high place
and remember unencumbered youth,
the freedom in not knowing
how quickly changes come and go
and I'll carefully pack that advice
with almonds and cashews,
with grain and white cheese

with less fat into a waterproof sack
because one could never imagine
poetry like this, or words put down
on paper lasting for more
than two thousand years, surely
they were drawn in pictures,
on smooth wet cave walls
and people were stick figures
without the power of reason. I'll
long for that black dirt because it's
something I can predict
in spring, summer, fall, winter
the only thing true happens;
in the now past, the moment
when I sat on a corner curb
and thought of existence
not because philosophy
was a discipline
but because I was tired
and needed to rest
with six-packs of empty
soda bottles and red cheeks
from exhaustion. What can
one ever understand about strong
minutes, short time when clarity
is overwhelming and baffling

and then startling back on two feet moving
to the grocery store?

An assistant in the editorial
department says in a boyish
voice, "We know you are looking
for something, so please know
this is a one time deal." Keep
looking, seeking, trying to find
what the mission essential is on earth
with its silver streaming sun
and turquoise Great Lakes
and slightly green ocean, salt
and rain leaves only salt water;
sailors put water in jugs along
with rum in case their fears ran
high after being on the ocean
for so long, looking for something
always mapping and dreaming
of solid footage, light shell-broken sand,
and fresh fruit or large nuts or berries.
They aren't ashamed that they
are looking, nobody can make
them feel bad about their quest
for survival when they're against
the storm, tempest sea; they

are not red-faced, red-handed;
they are not caught when trying
to make a living; they aren't pirates
but people with an ethic. Then go
to politically red Ohio, to the black dirt
and white faces tucked
into the barn; the barn door flew
open, and it wasn't a zipper down,
it was no joke; one can earn money
if one is willing to pay taxes, accept
tax cuts for the very wealthy; I'll
be in like Flint, Fred Flintstone
at the rock quarry. Carve everything
in stone. Carve your name. Etch
that you came to North Carolina
and became a seeker, looking
for authentic vocation, occupation,
a simple job on account
of multiple degrees; it is an ethic
to want to work in factories, in mills,
in furniture plants, but writers quickly
pass go attending real estate
class with fifty-something housewives
now working in department stores,
in cosmetics or fine jewelry
or household appliances with red plates

and mixers. It's the fate one has awaited
and it's waiting for me
if I lose several pounds and wax
two eyebrows, shapely and feminine. Words
won't work; they are only important
when they sell products like laundry soap.

Pull back. Words earn wages
for gabby indicted politicians
for morning editorial writers
who think great thoughts
and aren't busy in the afternoon
so they can chat
like a long distance phone call
from the lady in Ohio
or Missouri, from people
one rarely talks to and so share
details of shoe-buying sprees
and comfortable brands, high-class
shoes of poor quality, a worn hole
above the toe. Words are for hire
like carpet cleaners, tree trimmers
who know too that trees
aren't poems; the stately ones
fall come down for sidewalks
in front of homes, old

Friendly money mansions
with no young children
in sight; words are prosperous
in wills. claims, estates,
one will need to be exact
telling concisely what one means
to handpicked juries listening
to extents of injuries,
they're listeners, paid listeners
who fib out of duty
because they're busy mowing
lawns if they were not listening
to pitiful yarns stories
of unlucky plaintiffs
and resourceful defendants, words
can say when people witness
and remember details; the story
is made of accident reports
and fairies who see minutia,
a quick tip of a gray fedora
with a short red feather
from the strutting red rooster
let out of the barn
with advertisements on the sliding
door that slams against a frame
and close in, making insiders nervous

in small spaces without views
from the electric carnival rides, airplanes,
from scant air mountain lookouts,
from every high place
after the vision, the fast dream
on a sleepy morning in May; words
know what I'm thinking
once I find them; they tell
and they don't mind making salaries
if I'm very good, exceptionally
superlative fine or better than railroad
daring engineers when bandits
and masked men wanting treasures
for saloon gals, girls, women, ladies
and gentlemen come to the theater
to hear practiced lines
and to see well-timed tears
and they come to laugh deep belly
laughs and go home to silence
letting the yellow fat cat out
or hearing dogs bark
in the neighborhood. My words
have muscle, are strong
like malt liquor bulls
and champion herds moving
because the path is worn

to the barn, where buckets contain oats
and oats feed the young
on special occasions, when city visitors
come from far away. Words do
so much.

The teacher-poet taught
the many handout truth, a belly laugh
from the audience, clever reports.
I've heard that poetry deals
with the real tangible and abstract
in an imaginary way. Poets
are honest to a fault, the earth shakes
and heaves above them; California falls
into the ocean, a new coastline
is geologically formed overnight.
I've heard too much to tell exactly
what happened in the rural farmhouse
with the white barn, gossip
from little towns, villages
with uniform speed limits
for passing motorists. No one stays
at balcony shabby motels
or goes to the building downtown
to hear gray beat poets. The rooms
are unlighted; the guest poet corrects

practiced recited verse shaking his head
at mishap grammar in a key moment
when you are the word star
for being painfully honest.
The girl with the assistantship
says she doesn't believe
in any praise given in class; she
disagrees, she dissents
to pretty adjectives thrown
my way, disappointment
is mine and I can stuff
it into large fuzzy coat pockets
with bits of stray tobacco
and smoke on the steps
in winter, along
with the guy who never washes
his curly blond hair, and the women loved
him for his prose. Occasionally
he mattered, like all of us
looking for the mission essential
on earth, on any other planet
red or ringed with gases
where the people
have a few now minutes
and haven't evolved without ears.
The poetry class is extra

and nobody likes your real work
novel. Some are talking
of other lives, other circumstances
and who is to say if they lie?

Distant mild thunder sounds
like polished floorboards creak
at looking sleepless midnight
when the air conditioning turns on
and you're wide awake thinking
about day people's words,
in the dryness at the end
of the month; stagnant floods
are in New Orleans
and say that wasn't the rain
I intended with prayers, petitions
to a higher power, who sees all
knows all, and makes sense of the idea
that you know nothing, really zip
zero after years of education,
decades of experience
and a track record of being hardworking
and that's why one writes poetry
in silent afternoon, talking
about historical bandits
who jump between boxcars up

to the man with the safe's combination
or do they just blow the lock
to smithereens, to heaven?
Of course it falls back to the ground
a mangled mess
but the gold bars were fine
and worth their weight in butter
or is platinum the going concern
of prestigious credit cards,
meaning a borrower
makes oodles mega-bucks
and can't stay within a cash budget?
Don't worry about
accounts when words
can't pay rent or earn
a living wage. Bucks
aren't in the register, the till
like market bound white faces
coming in from rain;
it's pouring in OHIO, a deluge
too in mountain ranges for a few now
minutes, but one can't see it or feel
it because one stopped telling
the truth, worse yet admitting
it escapes when tightly pinned
down in a mile-long deep canyon,

not grand, just lost in doubt
and regret for trying to know
so much. The air is perfectly
still like people who are truly smart
and don't volunteer feeble nonsense.
Today, that word, a strong bull
intoxicating time-marker
makes one think what one said
was right on, was true, squirm
now or forever hold one's peace
squarely hitting straw targets
but please don't ever assert opinion
as truth. Opinions are for Saturday
newspaper readers, for cartoon lovers
gourmet bookstore coffee drinkers
featuring elephants and donkeys
with pack Native American blankets tiptoeing
around the steep turning ledges
and elephants carry Indian princes
through tiger jungles and crowded
roads.

Seekers

Truth gives one a soapbox
uneven letter activist's signs
and I can stand on the corner

and say loud bullhorn pontificate
to the harried unsuspecting
working world. It is embarrassing
to know so much for sure,
to be solidly convinced
with long passionate pleas
for others to follow
me who writes letters
to the editorial editor
even with the 30-day limit;
don't close fence me in;
I've an elaborate story to tell
and bystanders must listen
perk up ears to primetime political
speeches when approval
numbers are down, it must
make one down in the dumps
when one's sneaky sham rhetoric
doesn't sell and nobody believes
in what is put across
and the media corporation newspapers
don't mock but change
the subject when people
are about fed up, had it to here
on the wooden crate, speaking
high into the microphone.

Sages say it's never good
to be defended in a newspaper,
but Ralph Waldo
Emerson says don't worry
only bad repute is coming from people
who have made up their minds
from Ohio black dirt farmers
from church-going North Carolinians
from the Vermont Poet
Association where everyone
is glued to a seat with maple
warmed sugar; they're not happy
and the words are flowing
like hard water from the well
that white faces sip drink
after standing in the dry sun
from sunrise to sunset
and the form-conscious Vermont poets
could care less about Ohio
where ground is flat
like a deflated inner tube
and unchallenging
for gray-beard bicycle riders
who are also upset
in North Carolina
about a multitude of trucks

so be careful when one stands
in the street with a sign
be careful when I protest
fallen soldiers; some people
want sidewalks and on-time
school buses, want to fire
superintendents and defeat
board members at local dogcatcher
elections. And can I say
they lie? They know truth
about divesting stock, the truth
about Martha Stewart
at Camp Cupcake; they know
a thing or too about Enron
and bilking millions of pounds
of butter from retirement
accounts; but don't talk politics
unless one is prepared
for rebuttal; the therapist says
I can talk poetry, revealing
my innermost concerns
and don't say it has a thing
to do with the world
it's private, delivered
in a confidential letter
with CONFIDENTIAL printed

on the envelope; the truth
ran under the fence today again
and sleeps in a wingchair
upon designer pillow stacks
when nobody is looking
or is too preoccupied
to care about zealous school
board members in every town
the ones who graduated six children
from the system and know
everything for sure. Make
this person a friend, nod, eagerly
say "yes" and one is on the
way to never making another
wrong decision. Facts are involved
in decision-making. Emotions
make protest signs, travel to D.C.
to join with the Federation
to Free the Lost Seven, six or four
somewhere unfairly in rat hole jails
on the international scene.
I tell you citizens, registered voters
care when they know the truth
about one point stop sign ticket
or have tickets to swanky
sit-ins where Vermont poets

read from sunrise to sunset
and drink cool fruit juice
or martinis. I'm not telling
the truth because
Vermont poets do not leave
the Green Mountains
for country plaid furniture
or long uncomfortable tables
at dinnertime in winter let alone
for an outdoor festival; they're
words are classically eloquent
for nature and for mission
essential seekers who wait
for phone calls from books
editors who tell of the small
space on the pages; she'll look at it.
Essential seekers recite
resumes, vitas, emphasize
multiple degrees until they sound
against the frame, pathetic
in their own minds; so they
comfort soothe themselves
with the thought of being
the word star anyway, I'm
the word star on an important
journey, sending out poet honesty

to deadline workers
who aren't fond
of being bothered between
abrupt answers. O' pity
where did you go? I thought
you were half gone
like the heavy cloud cover
in the Carolinas today, that
intoxicating, vodka, kick-ass
word strikes again
with so much spunk
and urgency, today I saw
the light, knew the truth
in now moments, for a short
minute in a Piedmont village.

He says that I'm a ffffine writer
so you go to the empty October beach
in a road rough silver sports car
to find the beach windy
and the boats coming
into the marina. The sea
is olive drab green
and the horizon is periwinkle
like a rich man's middle name
a funny word, a nerd word

as I note land shelves, erosion
from the last hurricane
that took a couple
of shingles from a rentable
house with a walkway made
of treated wooden planks
one can know for sure
that one needs a vacation
are tired of sweet penniless
words; you were going to say
it is a blessing and it is a blessing
when the mood hits
to express yourself
to voice someone else's opinion
as long as there is an agreement
so a man with integrity
can stand at a podium
before a cheering
and applauding crowd. Tell
them the nation
is going to change,
is going to become fair
and just, just and equitable
like the Founding Fathers' idea
that all men are created equal;
the balance of the scales

of justice, the lady
with her bronze dress
open at the top, sexy, blind
reassuring downtrodden
peoples everywhere. The
beach was a vacation three
Eastern hours from home
where the dog
is tightly caged from growth
and cars are the buzz
with engine lights on
and three designer pairs
of soft cased sunglasses
in the locked glove box,
where letters
are occasionally welcomed
along with bills
in the bush-covered mailbox
and the sky turned aqua
above the horizon;
the sand wouldn't pack
but was loose, and we watched
the sandpiper's skinny legs go
back and forth; sometimes it
finds a shelled morsel
with its black pencil beak

and nods to the lazy pelican
beside us, and the thought
of word failure doesn't leave
my mind but camps out
with a bright burning fire
hot, high, dangerous
to think too much
about inadequacy,
about the fabulous things
one might do if one were
a tangled beard pirate
with short blue pistols
just back from a raid
and noisy coins
run through thinning
fingers, hands with jeweled rings
full of meaning, a life
so full of meaning,
and happenings not understood
but accepted, accepting county
fairs where men put out political
buttons in reds, greens,
and yellows, bumper stickers
show from rusty chrome, metal
indicating social status
or how much one is worth

after raiding government coffers
or the king's treasure chest,
after being shipwrecked
and tossed to sea landing
on an island with other mates
people who do not count
anymore, and I can say
that's not true, everyone votes
in democracy, in Walt Whitman's
aggregate religious society
more than a hundred years ago
and I wonder if belief
is cut in stone, if it was strong
like white face bulls
in Indiana, show me Missouri
or Wisconsin where statesmen
are progressive, buying homemade
fatty cheeses and footballs tickets
for a Northern team snowing
hometowns for Vermont poets
who never write propaganda
if they can help it; they're steeped
in tradition attending Robert Frost
meetings for writing societies.
The ocean is olive green,
the color of army uniforms

and rolls, slides, foams
back and forth to make-believe
justice because anything
is possible in the face
of beauty, and nature,
and God, that higher power
that lets one know one cannot
tell the truth on one's own
I cannot count on pirates
and railroad bandits
or people with integrity
when given mucho power
within the military industrial
complex, that 1950s, 1960s
stuff that applies
to a world losing compassion
and experience, and eloquent
Vermont poets who
are seldom political, in now time
until the times call prophets
and others of important words.

So you scribble an address
on a losing candidate's notepad,
sending out another resume
for thoughtful consideration

and I wonder why politics
pursues me and won't let
me turn away to a farm
or an ocean, petrified sharks
teeth are out the question
and now three years from fifty
I've many inquiries
to make of noteworthy men
who succeeded today
realizing mission essential
the same year seminary
was plausible
believable in my mind
and again I knew the truth
again for a month, a year,
in the daytime or nighttime;
something made me think
I could tell others
and I was wrong
while others were winning
prizes, exacting salaries,
and gaining titles
to impress investors too
material for truth. Wrong
can be absolute; I don't
need to be reflective, at some point

there is sabotage always
observations too keen for men
keeping jobs, passion
is scary to well earning,
excitement is for baseball games
where the bases are loaded
and the ocean is exquisite
to me, too amazing to be believed
too energetic, moving, swaying
making its point to me
without words, but I insist
and so come up with colors
and names of birds
because I've have to urgently
need to go back to Victorian
kitchens and a grandfather
that didn't drive to New Boston
drinking beers instead. Go
back to some root, an anchor
for pirate fantasies,
like one ever had a name
and needed a millions words
to make fuel take-off, lift-off,
whatever makes one go very fast
to fickle planet stars, fate destiny,
obsession, illness, and staying

within bounds, avoiding tickets
now.

The rain comes down for two days now. The illness scares
me and makes me wonder
about the future. I think my commentary is too liberal for
North Carolina papers. The audience is different than in the
Midwest also. I think they're more passionate, and
so are more difficult to get along with. But 1960s' liberalism
is out; it's unlucky to be
out of sync with the times. Minimalism went out with
Raymond Carver, and probably
will soon be back after college instructors have told students
to stress details. Details are all.

Adrienne Rich warned about silence
of its peril and she is right, correct, aye
to count the tremendous cost,
to pull out her international Visa
saying I can't pay cash
today. I can't come up
with president profile nickels and quarters
dimes: forget the pocket change
everyone wants new dollars
the monetary revolution
when slight hungry children

aren't fed, drugs cost too much
and are like unanswered silence
but it's not quietness
we pay for; it is the knowing
the same thing the first
human beings cast out for paper.
It is often knowing when situations
are wrong misunderstand the television image
trying paper bills, legal tender money
that can pay for substandard housing
shacks for rough roofs, noisy hot water pipes
for blue smoking air out of climbing stacks
with lights so airplane pilots
are sufficiently warned about colossal structures
about possible collisions midair tragedies
fog-related accidents earth revolving
so populated without caring kin
and others who can be called
in a tight pinch, when chest pains
and other physical body maladies
are the battle of the day
and we know solitary nothing
of time and her plans
and we can break the silence
but we can never pretend
to tell the truth, we can only know

half of the price and even Rich
says, she contends take it or leave it
the toll is inevitable while one wonders
about the steady rope stream of rain
in the concrete gutter moving
to where rushing drain water goes
after blinding downpours
after the holy deluge
nothing but record weather events
for days, nothing but subzero
for muted Moscow, for once warring Berlin
and passionate Russia cuts back oil supplies
for Finland: the message is
come along, cooperate or else wear
authentic fur muffs and scarves cover
the stinging faces of Red Square
and Cossacks in wool trousers claim
to absolutely know there
and of course knew nothing
but political doctrines and ideology
a nineteenth century manifesto for workers
when white dusty block ice is measured
in feet, in meters, and thickens
and people who knew
the exacted price of knowing what
was not popular and protests

not necessarily spoken, put on signs
but shown in giveaway glances
informed eyes are poor liars
even when they need
to be dull and stupid disinterested
bargain hunters bystanders making their way
to meat markets, the string tag shows.
Landscape planters are full
of dead resting leaves in January
and the strong lasting summer
will soon come with its lifted
bully heat; it is the season I dislike
the full weighty trees wilt
and people wear fringy straw hats
at noon in the middle of the day
like Asian peasants in a rice field
and the African air sweeps across
the Atlantic swirling
like a spoon in a coffee cup
or ideas on an anxious night
and all finally passes with the day
memory recollections of former
of history personal leather interiors
driving time into the future
as if it were a groove-wheeled tractor
in a muddy competition to pull

another at the fairgrounds
of youth a rodeo breaking bronco
and milky mashed potatoes
from the Presbyterian women under
a rust-colored canvas tent; the hucksters call
from chance game rows and everybody
wins today a teddy bear if one can look back
with clarity, with visual acuteness
or make sense of where one's
been in pink shaded houses with sidewalks
near grocery and drug stores
a mile away from the community
gem college, the Swedish
institution with anemic white faces
and proper well-spoken professors
tell texts and who know Shakespeare
in a farmer's, tiller's city
and the black rich earth until
we understand local history too
the land value corn crisp
making dark night rustles
in the July summer wind
worth large faded overalls on
callous skin muscular hands
weathered men talk at the feed storage
centers grain elevators and recount

other harvests sending children
to limestone pricy private colleges
so they can come home
and nobody understands farming
or philosophy but knowing
is the goal of worn fathers dutiful
and round mothers who staking
pride and stewing apples
for meals chicken fresh
eggs in the morning coffees houses
and guitar sessions in another
world that she brought life to
in birthing labor and see the hands
that know the azure earth safety
in knowing how vegetables
grow and how seedlings sprout
at noonday cold bundled against
elements without chemistry
or tabs calculations; how we
calculate and perfectly envision
the future expecting grass
to grow high ground cover in cooler spring
and love, sacrifice faith, pleasing
theater movies that do not last long
blue collar workers build portfolios
and anticipate falsely government

checks and will pay health
care life car insurance as the way
we live next to knowing
sweetly endowed Swedish colleges
we will be secure realizing
the sixteenth century artwork masters
seven naked ladies posing with cherub
from another era, the hot
flat summer will not be a friend
when the garden becomes dry
that is the cost of homely revolutionaries
of who reckon with wooden-handled hoes
and simple pruning autumn tools
and take defiance out in yard work.
An outreaching child will come home
and know more than generous parents
and that's the way life progresses
leaving solid legacies we call tradition
nothing changes from this equation
the oppressive heat is for six months
and it is the cost, the copper penny price
for lamb winters where the rain
falls instead of snowflakes.

I do not know Vermont poets
You can't say I'm guilty or complicit

or good enough to write verse for critics.
I don't know them so I imagine
that their rugged in-tune children grow up
to be ardent environmentalists
sitting in meeting halls with painted floors.
I don't know if stiff winter winds
blow through estate houses or if wood burns
cut from gray rust rotting trees, trees dead
and long stretched out across soft forest bottoms.
I can't be faulted for not knowing their choice
of drink simple dinners because we can only imagine
our closest or farthest neighbor we think
about weighty prestigious university theories
on how the earth turns, about religious texts
and we guess on the most important
aspects of existence and easily call out
and speak of inculcating knowledge to young
unthinking students dulled from images
unrelated to matching words with their objects
and now they don't understand us
we don't understand what modern media marvel
is in their brain. I only know what I read
in the newspapers. I only know what I hear
on television and the world splits in its sources
back to the dense machete land and the longest river
and indigenous drums, customs that mean

nothing to us. I wonder about your truth
that you write on the afternoon freight trains
by broken windows in a government legislative
building. I wonder if you've heard
we do not negotiate bargain play easy
with guns and now people silent; what do they
think? What are they suppose to say
in houses rubble in streets crooked
in fenced in areas where people spend their time
all day all night weeks months lifetimes
in wrecked ruined bulldozed shattered houses?
I do not know Vermont poets or the scope
of their concerns. Frosted apple orchards
are near ice glazed windows without storm glass
when the harsh season is boundless. Are poets'
clothes mimicked in catalogues and mail order
online and shipping costs rise and I've given
a credit card number for a chamois-like shirt
in heather? I told you I know nothing
about northern culture do not hesitate to speak
because ignorance assumes before it knows
without fully exacting the price of delivered goods
or services. Vermont poets are prophets with right
deep words and forceful lines. I think they might move
us even push forward if anybody heard their lines
almost too English pretty, but not too pretty if everyone

understood words. Authentic bards poets
talk to themselves and do not look
up words in the dictionary; its too late for that
meanings aren't universal and I, a Midwestern
poser: I might claim to know audiences,
but I only guess about Vermont poets.

I can only suggest they are not books.
Books are like years ago college friends
I expect nothing from them but a message
once a year when I remember sage whispered
thoughts coming into my ears like welcomed
waited for stories displayed on magazine racks
at the newsstands where people sip hot potent
bitter cups without liquor.

I occasionally want
a hefty volume to make me drunk with another's
words, falling down drunk when the keys are taken
away or hidden under the straw mat on the step
put above a narrow weathered doorsill.
I want books to reveal what I have never thought
of like how to scuba dive in paradise
how to change an overdue timing belt
how to cook for perfectionist chefs
for frequent restaurant goers fine suited

New York investors who keep the bottom line
and wear dime store reading glasses.
I often haven't read books
in a linear way looking for what startles
amazes like showy silk clad magicians
at advertised circus performances
high wire acts acrobats defying gravity
and planning for the future like seers.
I want books to tell me that I feel kinship
with the universe with cosmic hippies
and people considering what
it means to be at a crossroads turning
very fast in one direction skidding
on the brown puddle pavement
exacting speed space valorous intent.
I expect much from books
but I do not want them to sing melodies
or do things that are not for them.
I do not want them to plant radishes or tend
babies in the afternoon. I do not want
them to switch the shining river's direction
or make ponds fill into anglers' lakes.
I want companions with limits scope
describing planet Neptune journals
of scientific men agreeing with poets fine
about the moon starlight night words

at their best and books finally retire
go to sleep in board made shelves white
seen from the street in vague pictures.
I do not want to know everything they tell.

I do not know laboratory scientists
who might wear white coats
or beige Dockers. I could not understand
their articles on stem cells global warming
inescapable climate change. Their forecasts loom
for poll driven politicians to ignore the heating earth
for memory-lapsed middle-aged onlookers who never
believed in the establishment status
when they were young out of the slick
university tiles polished during lull times
when the students were in bars lifting
beers and preparing for tests. I imagine
scientists like poets have followers
and they walk down the hall with protégés
and assure them about graduate schools.
I understand nothing about tables. I guess
that scientists are masters of small talk;
esoteric experiments far out and not meant
for truck drivers, dry cleaners, workers
so they talk about hamburger joints
and write graph-filled papers that journalists

sleepily decipher after deadlines. They talk
about cat dog family pets and know nothing
about each other; the biologist is distant
from the methodical chemist and the weatherman
is not an astronaut. The drugs made today
will make you predictably sick with side effects
but the alternative is being sick
so FDA officials stamp approval
on high pressure systems mumbo jumbo
to increase credibility and ongoing belief
in the guess.

I do not wish to be known like mice
when the black yellow razor beak hovers above
circling the clandestine musings in town speak
about where you came from with your fake
country accent.

I did not come from a farm
in Ohio, and I do not know white faces
in the river valley where I used to play
in the hours before dark. Cows stood
on the river's steep flood eroded edge
and looked on at the boat, the city's
lights colored the water for miles. You
can be known for great talent

even talent finds its enemies
because it is dangerous to stand out
the patterned butterfly is pinned and cased
for elementary children and no one ask
whether it should've been special unusual
Know it might have said yes for short glory
the bright moment when a concise word hits
the page, the arrow pierces targets
and love is returned. I do not know
if glory is worth a pound of green grapes
on sale in the summer market. Glory
deceives the one who jumps into battle
and only half dies with useless legs
so much for courageous intent
and the dreamy butterfly knows the cost
of flying into nets, the cage, prisons
of being closed into the barn awaiting
a trip to the feed pens; young white faces
are kin to beautiful beings fate deals
a losing tragic lot and they no longer climb
hills in illusions of freedom unheard
of fences in ephemeral awareness.
I 'd rather have a pound of grapes
than appear to have knowledge
in front of those who confidently
expound spin speaking as broadcasts.

Still I might put my grapes into a basket
and imagine a light wine
a wine that is not troublesome
making every occasion a celebration.
I do not know but I can hope
like the slightly living rose bush
in February. I can hope to remember
trying events and travel destinations
of exactly how my life has unfolded
of how I have missed out lamenting
miscalculations destiny errors as if one
affects a journey through space and time.

I want to sleep on rainy nights only hearing
the drops cover the green stems
of spring waiting. I want you to ride in my car
and never question the speed of
a heist-like getaway. The world revolves around
the sun keeping equilibrium in its hurried
pace. I see no reason to stay in place
awaiting Midwestern scenes. I tell you
now that we can love and not know. It's
the simplest endeavor and requires little
reflection from burning stars. One can
await uniformed couriers delivering books
letters from overseas and watch as they go by

speeding in secure trucks backing
into driveways rushing to doors with large
packed boxes. Come with me now, today
and let's be heroes recognizing
when the wasted undeclared war is lost
whatever we imagined will not happen
here and there is no point in staying
to look at missed opportunities.
I cannot wonder about how time links us
to fads so one is outdated and comment counts.
But come with me today seeing a strong
common word show its urgency. Ah, we are alone
you say and ancient philosophers sit on stumps
while bony romantics disagree seeking
to cover up that passengers are moot
and harbors are unsafe when booted pirates
whittle whistles to call on thugs. Come
with me now today; this is the now verse
and these words this jazz is not wisdom
can only suppose the workings tacked
to the board. If we're alone there is pretense
and we can live out vineyard patience while
darkness sweeps the gray from twilight
hours, and I show you all I've witnessed
about home.

I do not know Ohio farmers. I see them
riding tractors across fields from the road.
I suppose the land is a legacy, and the farmer
calls his tract home. It is where animals
are animals without sentimental ownership
or names. They come and go to sustain permanence
lifestyles. Cats are special and live in sliding door
barns to keep down mice birds unsuspecting.
Farmers are kind in their own way never shying
away from pragmatism and know what needs
to be done for the day. I do not want pragmatic
love scripted and without nonsense. A time
without folly should be short laughter persists
throughout trials when the mind could turn
as rough as skin weathered in the drying wind.
I don't know that for sure. I see these people
with simple political opinions; they visit
with elected officials at county fair booths
and never think of Lincoln or Grant or civil
wars the past is gone to farm workers tilling
land as flat as an ironing board. If they are
in trouble the community exists as a yesterday
prop. I guess they suspect they are as alone
as twentieth century thinkers but they do not think
these thoughts when the hay is cut.

Small Boats

I can tell you about my home grown over
and a grapevine tangle on the single wire fence
and nobody farms and nobody answers phones
or doorbells. People walk in and leave messages.
I can tell you I learned football plays in the side
lot and took V-bottom boats to where the river
was encroached with poplars and it gave off reflections
of its dense borders. I followed the pastimes of old
men who lived in unpainted porch- covered cabins
and caught catfish. I did not know them but heard
their names from others. Small boat motors
were on stands waiting for repair, and I waited
to leave, read books to leave, imagined the life
of an educated recluse with no pond. When
I came back I claimed nothing and wore white
blouses and yellow shorts gave up sweatshirts
and for a while I could not love the river. I could
not love the past and it was gone.

I take everyone I love there.
It's a precedent and they stand
on a concrete seawall seeing the sights
freedom and discontent. I think they should visit.
Water laps the blowing wind makes the river
run backwards. Currents take one away

and one cannot swim against broad
motion never ceasing never apologizing
for carrying trees like Viking ships.
I want you to know the cost in slime mud
in landmark dive tavern marinas blistering tar
roads. I want you to come with me
when we leave and guess a leading part in a play
in another time. Distant past is theater.
It wins an award for just showing up
in altered evening gowns prom dresses
below a massive chandelier. I find my ideas
for books here preserved for onlookers during
floods rough-sided jacked-up houses built on stilts.
We can go now to jewel Swedish colleges
and try to know diagramed botany, the lesson
of plant fertilization and children myths.

Happenings go without musings
and leave dryness, dusty, unobserved
events and inadequacy is felt, in memory
in stilted words coming too easy. One can rage
against flint hardness, the sharp callous scope
of numerous chatty witnesses, of numerous
buzzing injustices mounting abstractions
confusing staying with one's sentences
until the end of sighing. I can tell you

I've tried too hard, stout romance's puppet
for three decades. It's not so simple: someone
should have said loudly after tapping rapping
my strained head and hearing its brains clatter
in the cupboard where I keep the big tea
cup with authors' faces; their names
below the image. I do fault the paper
for not making people understand what
it took to get to the office supply store
origins are unimportant matters. Yesterdays
are for thin-lipped historians smoking pipes
in rising blue compartments for buffs touring
the long line of monuments and camera-clad
tourists aiming focus on gossipy war boots
and a broken dish.

I do not blame time. Time is innocent
like the full chalky blackboard waiting
to be erased so eager teachers can start over. I
see no earthly reason to pick on space;
there is only so much room; greedy intellects
take it all like the bank robber when the vault
opens and there is small quarters to fill
the leather suitcases and catch the train
out of town before the law comes down hard
searching streets alleys car lots restaurants.

Cops want the paper and to give back what
was stolen from another. Relics recall
when the money is found ten years later
underneath the rose garden at the corner
church. I say you can fool bad guys
and good guys as a collective because paper
can't help it but it lies and never knew the truth
while the lights shine through a tree encircled
neighborhood yard owned for ten years
by a freewheeling chemist and his wife.

Bandits are a Hollywood construct
like deer pioneer ice statues in Minnesota's
warmest January. We see the tugged at
loss and claim fiction yarns tales make believe
when we know we could never let any
of it go on our own. We couldn't say "Take
it," I am glad. The man with the covered
face and short gun is part of our imagination.
I do not know him; his essence slips slides
when broad yellow rays heat pavement
turning playful faces red so that they blister
after the mild short months after New Year
in St. Paul or Minneapolis or near boundary
waters where metal bark canoes are carried across
boggy woods onto another nameless lake

and the untested water is fine for drinking
and food is put in the trees at night so bears
thieving animals don't take it in the dark.
I do not know thieves or what they want
with paper backed up by the treasury, what
they want with paper for business newspapers
telling of American carmakers lay-offs. I see
paper when orders are decreed and when
accounts are settled little slips and when the
carwash accepts certain codes. I've seen hideous
blank paper try to negotiate with timid words
held to their surface; the words want off
good bye because sense tells that communication
isn't a primary job and no one
will want packed sentences of the robbed
because of well placed letters. Words are solitary monks.

I've never seen a pirate; one supposes they steal
from government ships, the King's ship
and some royal Navy officers swing down ropes
wishing not to walk the plank. The plank
strikes me a bit odd but it is the nautical movie
way men are punished on boats. One supposes
too that they are chained below until wrists bleed
and the pirates claim victory after treasures
are opened which might be hearts if the measure

weren't gold. I've multiple degrees loving words
and word stars from poetry class and everybody
oohs and ahs when they do the dance today
and knives aren't between the teeth and poets
don't fear drowning but the dead silence
of disapproval after one drives very fast
to school contemplating an audience of
young people. I'll be their matronly aunt
and know why red apples are red
and turnips are like white and purple radishes
and they will mock me when the hour is over
for saying too much about scantily dressed
pirates living near the water and poets living
by the water catching the surf yet another way
to walk the plank turning tan while marine
biologists collect samples of sea water testing
its saltiness. I'll be the old salt man fishing
from the pier and students assume I know
tides and little else beyond the illness in my knees
and they will ignore me until I'm featured
in verse. I'll be the child lost in motion
carrying sand buckets and laughing
at waves unaware of pencil-legged birds
and parents smelling of lotion and beer. I
will never be the point of a poem because
the poets are young and children are distant

ideas not yet full of pathos. I think I know
young poets, but you've probably guessed
that I lie like paper unwilling just to stop
to quit saying like Vermont elders
who are the prophets and would never write
about being the old woman in a
large family picture, but one can hear
much when one is invisible; the people
do not mind speaking and they do not mind
outdated kin who couldn't tell the names
of pop stars and who don't know what's going
on in Manhattan, the latest in rent
or what people do in a city what they do
in the country after they've fled
to a better location. The tide comes in
and I sit on the apartment rocks
with my almost multiple degrees dreaming
of time and how she's always a girl busy
with retreating sand and nets
for nothing but the fall of water through the weave
no prison, no chains, no plank, a linear
rush, a straightforward movement without regard
or care. Time visits paper and leaves the doors
open, the dishes out, the bed undone forever.
And poets will wince but that is the cost
of imagining against something as real

as time and the messy houseguests whose
prints are on the floor in Georgia red mud
of the clay pot persuasion, Cherokees on
their way from home. I can't say for sure though.

Specialist doctors say they don't know for sure
reading MRIs and ordering blood tests.
Uncertainty suspends illness in thought
while it exists in a body losing its health
and I can drive very fast down curved
tobacco two-lane highways, very fast
never knowing if one can negotiate
the sharp turn with a full-sized automobile
from Wendover. I feel like I could tell
you what I want from words now
and I might fail to give them due respect
deserved honor because of my own inability
to say it right. My perception isn't clear
and I think I've been discouraged
about their uses in the world; words work
from fire stations, with elevated electrical
workers. They're prominent in hospitals
and other places where people utter
needs, requests for healing. I see flocking birds
as a sign of holiness and wonder why the scenes
matter to me. Doves and white pigeons

both stretch gliding across
state lines interstates are not the easiest
way to go fast, for words to tumble, going
on their ends to create understanding.
I saw a retriever watch a quail from a window
intently, never taking its eyes from the bird
and they might have been friends, and they
might have stayed in the backyard woods
if the hunter did not come between them.
Our instincts look for healing, words
are the arbitrator and go into
whatever madness we've adopted
in the beating heart on road abandoned Sunday
when small buildings ring
and gladness touches souls and other real
notions like sturdy faith that can only
be to the grasping keeper like the eyes
holding the keen hunter's prey on the post.

I went back, turned back, a pilgrimage, a way
to childhood roots, the stained glass,
the curved door, heavy dark wood
where the saints formerly lived
with their weighted drape-like robes
and calm somber expressions
as if they knew they were the church's

chosen. They have to be good and perform
a miracle. They were the examples, models
for young people who were impressionable
and thought that holiness
was as long and shadowy
as beams across the sanctuary.

I went to the grotto, where a Hispanic woman
and a five year-old saw the Virgin Mary
\and told the newspaper; people came
from miles around filling the parking
lot of a riverfront restaurant. The cameras
descended, and some said they saw nothing
but were believers, others want to believe
like I do in more than ordinary life,
the blue robe Our Lady of Lourdes, Our
Lady of Kernersville and Moline,
every miscellaneous town along the river
and along the interstate who makes
herself known for celestial purposes
who rarely visits for naught. I prayed
to her after penance, as a child
can admit error, mostly made up,
mostly surfacing in adult life
for truth because nobody likes it
and eventually the truth makes its path

into light. It comes to where others
can see it, and there aren't apologies,
except those given on steps in front
of three-storey brick school buildings
and perhaps one will have to testify
and maybe not. It is nice to be trusted
again after years, after the time
goes by and a young woman writes
and comments about news stories.

I used to know but cannot claim
truth now after the swirl of color
after the many, many squares
of retold stories put together
with what? I guess glue or steel
or lead or invisible words,
pictures without words. The
cross stands out, the Catholic
grandmother who believed
that everyone had something to bear
and unbelievers can be unbelievers
because catastrophe doesn't happen
and men escape the meaner qualities
in living, the poor are devout
in foreign countries where wealth
is not and too obvious, where cars

and four bedroom homes
aren't in real estate sections
for all to see, admire until
witnesses are sick with inadequacy
and greed. My faith is resilient,
weathers the speeding wind
that blow down parts of weaker trees
leaving the trunk and spindles.
I've tried to take hold of this feeling
when the soul is placid and all
is well and all shall be well
when the grotto Lady stands
under the lights of the river
a playground, where the catfish's
smooth skin slides through
water and people are brought home
to look. Oh, but we can't be sure.

We can't sure about any particular holy
place among sinners; then where
should the truth come? Who needs
love more than drunken fools
and riverboat captains, the gracious
servants who are lost in business
who would come home if they were called?

I gave my mother a rosary
and she said it was to her liking
with iridescent beads aqua and green.
I wonder what she thought
on that Good Friday, her face said
she was full with unexpressed words
the sounds we hear in our minds
the sorrow we do not share
the love we've perhaps forgotten
in rituals and pageantry in being
with others who might suspect
our uncomfortable seat before
the Lord. Yesterday I slept all day
and was up at mid morning. I make
no sense of the hours unconsciously
spent in riddling dreams
and afterthoughts and no way
to drive home with the roads
jammed with trucks. The risk
might be worth it through mountains
driving fast, keeping steady, and
why does no one call when half
applauded and the other half were
silent? If they called would they say
that they missed me, would they call
me talented, brilliant and it was

a mistake to force me out even though
I quit? I want the audience to know
what plain darned happened and why
I put down my pen and why
I want the porch light on
in the summer, so people can see
through the thick trees. I tire
of looking through window glass
and seeing only various green, only
the two mini-vans and a woman
gardening with yellow gloves.
I drink coffee now and the teapot
is still and whistles no more. The
world should know, this knowing
is important, is crucial, is exacting
but I cannot tell you anymore.
I planted grass seeds in the springtime,
more green, and I long for the
colors and a horizon, a large sky,
with brown, and faint sunshine on
white hay. You tire of my homesickness.
It is all I shall speak of now. I've done
the national lecture circuit to applause
and find I want to go home
and rest without a special name
but as one who has worked hard

and as one who has given while
others have been professionals
and secretaries, have typed a million
words and have loved a dictionary.
I want precisely not to be rich
but to carry daily food to two dogs
who sit outside my door waiting
for human contact. That will not
be much to ask in the future.

Today, I decided that I want
too much, indifferent time ticks on
and stop it or control
what it gives. Time never promised
me anything so why should I be dismayed.
It is not the slightest trouble
that the clock's hands move around
forever, never noting that people
observe when they move past a number
and peace could happen today,
if leaders willed it so. The killing
could stop in days, in hours, in minutes
if the right minds willed it with black
neckties and state plates, long speakers
until everyone wanted to go
home, resting, retiring, giving in

to gray clouds of smoke
the bargaining red chip
on the shiny smooth floors
of deadly remembered malls
and swanky restaurants.
Today I thought it might begin,
the silence of a rising mood,
the hot tangled but cold rubble
powder ashes tired and without heat
or life whatever moves a person
to pity or repugnance over loss.

Creeds

The kitchen television was silent
and no news came, no mouth
spoke creeds and declared opinions
until the cord spit from the wall
about all the knowing
and pretending that people
do when they cannot know
for sure. I can talk like
that and show off my language,
verbs spew from my tongue
and I understand action,
what soldiers do on alley streets
and from vacant buildings.

I know the papers that are signed
under light blue ties and flag pins
for the betterment of the ages,
action, I might understand it
if it were well intentioned
and for restoration, a return
to what used to be in public affairs
when food was plenty, abundance
was in the pantry, in drawers
with clean socks and in gas guzzling
SUVs. I only know what we used
to know and now it does not pertain
to the present or history
but forward events marking
the bounty of dreaming consumers
picking up where someone left off.

Mighty Israel is defending itself
with forward movement
and the world watches the rockets
hit Lebanon. All concrete crumbles
in front of the global community
and we are shocked at destruction
and detached, and far away, dry
faced and the interested parties
know one poisoned truth or a another

one story or a couple. Who can
say? Who will say which country
intrudes invades marches into
foreign lands? It is too much
and one should never want
for the birds to know how badly
the earth is torn. Time let us rethink
the possibilities, an alternative
to bloodshed for real, like when
the mockingbird sings in the night
and the chickens come home to roost
and when the robins return in the spring
and the bluebird makes its country home
you will see beyond the devastation
and your occupied mind will suppose
that it knows the fair sky
where creatures fly wanting nothing
but abrupt change, revolution
of beginnings of quietness
and well being or health away
from the desire to speed past
blacktop highways and yellow
line and they want sweet ample rain.

The bucket-poured rain is overlooked
and cannot cool the burnt earth

when weather is not a problem.
Don't complain about heat any longer
unless your heart is stone broken
into sand, like in the towel
of a beach bum. Shake it off,
the problem, the approved carnage
washes like the sea, seeming natural
to those who watch the waves
arrive with more and more power,
the ability to carry or drop aquatic life
in its tedious rush. The sea
is bored with breathing objects.
You foolish children wade out deep
as if some tender eyes protected or
even cared. Run with presumption,
scurry off quickly from false lovers
and journalists with right and left-handed pen.
Take your trust with you. I could call
you out and we'd keep our pistols in a
velvet-lined boxes and then we'd walk ten
paces and turn, fire, and, fall, then we'd stand
up again and repeat the silly game
because our leaders aren't statesmen
in motorcades; we are just playing a game
like they are tinkering with death
and who they call does not stand up again.

There is no comfort in war. We can only
stand far enough away that we can pretend
not to know the damage. This is great
advantage to contrived stupidity; we
aren't made to show disapproval
and say we are innocent and perhaps
we are for never pulling pins
or planting mines, for never launching
a missile. Our hands are clean, our laundry
is stacked in piles away from the commotion
the locomotion of explosive events
and revenge.

I'm bored with green. I admit that my car
goes too fast. I'm homesick and am
without position. The poet has no place
in the world besides Vermont, and I've told
you about that. My words baffle me, and I doubt
their verity. I like rain and to talk about birds
and dogs. I go back to Catholic grandmothers
and talk about truth, have the guts
to summon the word, call it up
like it were a spirit. I tell you over and over
again that I can't say for sure and know very
little. Have you loved me for this?
Do you understand me, putting it all together?

My long poem, my discourse, my treatise, is too
heavy but I will lightened for you, whom I
do not know and cannot name. I will speak of clarity
and show you the greatest boldest river
in the dew morning when it is as flat
and as mysterious as a film negative. Water
falls from my fingers and drops freckle
my hands. There are no drunken captains
but gentle old men who fish on the riverbanks
with worms from under the abandoned plywood
in a grown-over lot. The lot is tame though
and nothing that lives there bites, like you
complain of the melancholy in my verse.
Do you remember loving a man, a woman,
or some commitment that would last?
Did you ever put a ring on your finger? I think
you like the way ice cream runs down a
cone and the squirrels that hop from the
trash bins at a favorite university. I think
you are probably kind, bald, growing bald,
and somebody's uncle. I will not make you real
because I want you to hear me out and I'll try
to make it all more pleasant, and I'll not talk
of war.

There is a ceasefire and sides claim victory;
people wait out the silence to see if its true,
if the bombs stop dropping and soldiers stop
falling. I told you there be better news if you
could wait. People sigh and children are found
in the streets still wandering orphans until
somebody finds them. I promised you a happy tale
and I'm a tale-teller. I haven't one scent of
your favorite aroma. I cannot give you what
you want most: words that don't cheat. You
want to hear clear bells pealing for towers
on university campuses and she said she'd call
but hasn't yet. I won't wait by this phone
for it betrays me with a foreign voice
a person who wants me to consolidate my college
loans, neat like the sundial on a shady day. I tell
you on a day when the sun shines time
is eternal and no trickster. The phone offers
a cheery voice but tells no jokes, seldom
laughs aloud or reads verse to me. What use
is it then? It is to sit by, to carry and ring
in the parking lot. The war is over
and now there are only telephones to worry
us, to go off in some chosen melody when
driving very fast to the place wherever
we were going, and our pocket chatters.

The telephone has a mechanical voice
it works all day; it screeches, it turns,
it propels, it moves along so quickly
that I catch it like the clouds in front
of the moon, when it is bright and full.
Complaining serves no one, and suppose
I did find position, suppose I did find
worth outside of chronicling the damned war
and telling about the fickleness of words?

Word Star

I want to tell you that I love you
like I've never loved anyone before
of course my love list is long
and is full of catastrophe. But let's
not mourn the fallen roses in winter
or the way the sun retires without dread.
Let's not be sad. I know nothing
that grief can give; it is an empty vessel
and before long we'll forget
that there was goodness not ephemeral
not like a feather swaying through air
on a lost day. It's time really. That is
the message, that is the mission essential
that everything is today, now time.
Tears are yesterday's passion and today

is full of goodwill, tender thoughts
and soft ripe wishes under the streams
of river stars dancing stepping out
in the glowing evening restoration
is at hand the gruff with well worn
fingers at a machine for over twenty years
and today is my favorite and my charity
extends throughout noisy pounding rooms
or eight hours at the combine shop
when there are five years to retirement
and the heart leaps at only rest. I love
you when people want their rights
and the country is led astray
and all patriots feel it's too late to
make it right, the way the left arm
swings the hammer or stick. I love
you in the most simple manner
on the brightest day glowing
or the darkest minute in old life.
Private sentiment is fine; no one
can talk of war or guns or clothes
hiding flesh from enemies. The world
is full of enemies, people who don't
like each other when driving very
fast past country white faces
with advertising of a tobacco product

on a sliding door. I still love you
and try to connect the elements
the lines the dots the faraway emotions
that come to me when O poetry
captures my bird in the fist tight
and unaware, not knowing, never
knowing swindling words or spiral
staircases. Now should I explain
what never can be told? Please
don't question my words now
after I've told you about my heart
and please don't wonder about
the value of poetry when we are so
far away. I croon a little
and will not discuss world affairs.
I've my 24-7 obsessions with time
and how long it's been
and long it will take to erase bad luck
when the mechanical phone rings
from out of area, that green space
home addressing nice letters
and pretty greetings, my sister, and
when many several doors close does the house
burst open like a firecracker, unravel
because people in power know too much
and today, today, an important court case

was adamantly considered unconstitutional
and the deep red dahlias bloom and fade
according to the six month summer swelter
today not feeble impotent yesterday
was abundant in sunshine and no sign
of slow steady rain in puddles wet socks
and they say I am better at this expression
than any pedagogical fiction is a lie
and how many lies have I told
so the brass-handled door wouldn't slam
and the rattling mice wouldn't creep
around dusty dirt musty hard covers
in white bookcases on white walls?
I constantly wait. I dream. I suppose
many high-minded ideas in thoughtless
actions busy with children chores
and appointments. I could not
impress the gatekeepers; they sensed
my hesitation and noted my worry
when the myrtles bloom late
and the lighted slant of September rays
kiss the ground above leaves drying
my eyes commotion my interstate in sight
on the way home to the river's brown
might and conclusion. I'm alive
and weary.

Nature battles all; it duals and fights
back it will not go to sleep with harsh
words so it often speaks of peace
the way the snow arranges itself
on mountains when the crystal is blue
and red and blue drawing sight
into focus and I showed off my peculiar
steps in my starched creased striped blouse
for I had no suit, so silk scarf, no pin
or heels.

The position came and left me in loss
it is the greatest fight letting the poplar
leaves fall. The battle is not a war
in the usual sense; the bombs do not fall
but it must be endured like the heat
and it will wane although wishful thinking
and optimism stop by my house
and seldom stay. I promised you a better
story and there is one if you look into my purse
with the white soothing cream for skin aliments.
Why should I speak so hackneyed so trivial
when I'm trying to explain the exact nature
of yellow tired leaves making off from the stem?
It is a perilous escape and deer free of the hunters

when wind whooshes through gutters
eaves, and a country dog's scant fur becomes thick.
I will have no regrets and will smile
and end this obsession about occupation.
I turned it down. The world is occupied
and cannot be bothered; statesmen make off
with the bandit's booty being stellar
and principled. Principle will confuse
you and every refusal can be about a lofty
order, the conscience of kings and public
servants who dine on gold-trimmed plates
bestowing honor on loyal mediocrity
on simple fellows who like to gab. I love
it because the company is fine, and the
hours speed with peppery wheels over
desert roads where the heat radiates
like fumes; the desire is the problem
and now it is September, who can say
when the weather will turn teasingly cool
when the engine is hot and black suited
men still preside over fabulous meals
with straight crisp white shirts decorated
with fire engine roses wilting no more.
This is the perfect story I've told you
about and were you listening
as deaf conductors who remember yesterday

with an ear's memory? Do you care
about lost hunting seasons when the deer
runs away from predators and armed
men and women with full grocery sacks
come upon the scene, and there are hearty
feasts when the cooks work in stainless kitchens?
Nature can tell you, call and wait upon
your sterling guests with loose dollars,
a beauty queen's ransom. Kings and queens
do matter here losing no authority on
account of dining officials who bet
on the fawn's fate in cushioned forests.
Blame it on September, the quick way
that walkers move when a chill waits
for its day. I call this poetry, the mix
of words in patterns unknowing
and unknown to onlookers with glances
over surfaces like countertops
and the level of shining liquid in tumblers
or house ware glasses in sets, coming in
a pack of eight. I term this poetry, the word
dances through parades, digs for meaning
when it eludes the smartest brilliant
people.

I truly did not asked you to come here

and see how the sky clears and Pluto
is left abandoned by scientific engineers
who seldom chat with quarrelsome neighbors
over overgrown weeds in the neat nearby lawn.
Why do I talk about chatty men and celestial
bodies in half sentences making exacting
professors wince? You came here on your own
so don't accuse me of being obscure.
I learned verse around a table and sought out
praise from divas and egotists. Are you surprised
that I would tell you that, you whom I barely
know, who comes to my poetry with rules.
I broke the rules of poetry while bearded bards
were watching and yet none cried out thinking
it not worth a tirade, a diatribe, a rebuke. Blame
hesitant September or a month that pleases
you but is of no matter. The rebel knows
his cause and what must be done when food
covers every inch of a dining room table.
Nature will not deceive you and you'll know
who you are after the revolution if you decide
to participate, but do not accuse my verse
for it is honest.

The world finds its verity in newspapers
with happenings in faraway places.

I look for it in texts and imagine
that well-considered words contain
what I shall never know beyond my bleating.
So are you distant from me now, because
you wanted too much that I could not give?
Distance senses its place and never stops
from trying to separate us. I wouldn't lend
it a dime for identifying space. People
write to me from out-of state, and I answer
their letters quickly, much in the same manner
that lightening strikes, zigzagging in trucks
across West Virginia mountains, the turns
will amaze you, and I'll try to tell you
a folktale of no importance other
than someone spoke it before. I like stories
that are passed down from others
even though they have confused me
for I've thought they were true
and not entertainments. Do you know
or have I told you that most tales are meant
to wholly delight; bliss isn't correct
to the seriously downtrodden. The stories
can't be easily told, and we can revel
in hard facts like the stone of a courthouse
or of a gray statue in the empty square.
I talk very big for some who knows

little about a stranger's plight.
You are the one I've always known
and are no more familiar than New York
or the bustle, the taxi drivers, the food
venders. You are the invited
and the one who sees bars on the doors
keeping out feeling like the light switch
ushering in square dark places
where I might stumble
banging into walls black with the night
new in the day and manageable. How
do you love me now, who can only love
barely with a dull pain in my side
changing my usual awkward gait
for fear of pulling muscle
pounding like my restless heart
with no takers? And now I give
you my stories, the forgotten ones
in dreams that go like past reality
but what is that really, a truth for today
when the voices clamor and excite
in vindication and assuredness
of a certain but concrete moment
when elements come together
leaving one alone like the house
on a quiet morning on an uncomfortable

couch with the dog sleeping in a forbidden
chair.

Could you take me or leave me?
Indifference steals, creeps into
our affair, and I knew you wouldn't stay
long once you heard about other's tales
with saliva harmonicas and folk guitars
low melodies, off-beat strumming ballads
home or studio recordings the way you move
when the sweet sway hits the autumn trees
when they have gloriously lost their green,
thank goodness that eventually
they lose that monotonous color.

Ice Castle

I will build an ice castle
with gables porches
circular foyers
long carved stairways
to slick foreign tile
seal the windows
the doors with water
from a garden hose
better for roses
it is a bitter prison
that will melt
before the masses
the cheering audiences
in balcony seats
cell tight closed solid
situated in air
in the Southern sun
now its openings shine
flow into streams
like the rushing
of a springtime river

on a strong hiker's way
a steady gait firm
brown cedars
asleep from the season
before flowering trees
make dogwood hoes
the crooked handles
and the night is over
it does not hold anyone
its shrinking locks break
with glittering warmth
ardent fiery yearning
at last finally to be free.

When I Return

If I could remember
my whole life
and put it in front
of me like a road
through Kentucky
where the cedars
grow marching
along the blacktop
in communities
in the shade
of the sycamores
white patchy
memories come
and they go
they are happiness
after the sun
goes down
behind the trees
and the water is clear
always familiar
it is the same

when I return
in stump coves
in a song
or written word
see the pieces
what I can put together
after time dulls
wise certain sayings.

Churchgoers

Language of the heart
compassion discernment
the dark night of the soul
words church people use
they are kind enough
but never know
how to say, "no."
These people haunt me
shadows step close
stand next to me
monk silences meditation
singing songs chants
for everyday goers
who work for the homeless
in urban headquarters
some watch children
after years of politics
scholars graduates
I feel let down
no promised holiness
no prophets or saints

Why should I care
about motivation
question credibility?
The steeple can be seen
from the East and West
from the street sermons eloquent
and intelligent. I will
not be Thomas
who needed to witness
proof to believe.

Blowing Rock

The breeze felt
like birth
exactly freeing
the body
from heat
wetness
that could go
on forever.
Strollers
pass with infants
safe and secure
tied into movement
the wheels
hopping
over steppingstones
The old couple
sit on the park
bench waiting
for a new scene
they are onlookers
and the world

is a sight
of children
on shoulders
and people on
their way
to art fairs
down slanted roads
to silver jewelry
and photographs
of barnyards
and snowy landscapes
too unbelievable
for summer
where mountain
men sell apples
at roadside stands
the turning road
going home.

Helen

She irons clothes
and welcomes
her daughters to church
where the family
sits in the same pew
I've known her
for years
and she is comfortable
with card games
and coffee
in the morning
with friends who chat
about bedspreads
and curtains
who make small talk
and go to Sunday
school. I think
she is sincere
and does not care
who wins elections
life is simple

life is holy
life is done right
when the offspring
brings the salad
and the husband
is away from home.

Prediction

I will come apart
like an old shirt
soft warm checkered
sophisticated flannel
elbows wear thin
two bony points break
through the seasons
winter collar frays
at its natural crease
there is a hole
under the arm.
A button comes off
then another
two sides fly in the wind
separating flapping
the torso exposed
the sleeves shrink
from the dryer
and go around
with electric socks
eventually I become

squares for dusting
fine slick furniture
high oak woodwork
that darkens the room
making it sober
even with white paint
call it destiny
the way material things
are supposed to go
no secondhand use
or a sad trip to charity.
I will be given another
chance transformed
into cleaning rags.

Easter 2009

Tongues of flames
on mountaintops
the maples upward
the eye follows
the day into Easter
red buds growing
from rock cuts
along highways
the image changes
into a holy face
when I was lost
between interstates
sign problems
of going anywhere
across borders
plowed fields
the people I love
delivered in dreams
the mind solves
its own island maze
and settles for rest.

Omen

Sooner or later
you will know
what will kill you
the cough
the leg limp
the extraordinary
pain grief
and it will not scare
you because
you've seen it
for years.
It has chased
you in the dark
until the day
the clear vision
of freedom running
from the tremor
from the ache
prescription
glass in the junk
pile before

you wondered
about mortality
and the people
who care
about you
the long scar
stretching across
the abdomen
and you will
see it after surgery
the thing
that will do you
in put you
in the grave
the telling years
you know them
well tough rugged
ending.

Process

The going back and forth
the limbs move carrying
the directions for the machine
with the wheels rolling
and the plastic gears
of a child's contraption
or toy that goes from here
to there. The sun touches
the horizon line and tells
of morning until the scene
is old, the words older
and yet it watches the earth
and its mechanical trip
around recipes tucked into
boxes on the counter
or stored in a red and white
book above the stove.
The stand up mixer whirs
without batter, it takes
the steel around, its sounds awaken
coffee drinkers on the way

down the steps to the smell
of work, spent old, dirty rags
trying to make something
into a product that can be packed
into crates, shipped over rivers,
driven to markets, minted
coins drop into registers
and feel cold in pockets.
I wanted it done,
so I ask you for a ride past
traffic wondering how to get
from here to there without
taking the steering wheel
to drive. *

*Previously published in the Hollins Critic Vol.46 No.3 June 2009

Millennium

Afflicted hearts pulsing back blood
to the brain
and eyes. Make sense
of what you see here,
of gangster meanness
the gait attached
to swinging fists. Look
for yours, hear it
its strained resolve for remedies, leaves
and potions. Disembodied
organ, memory
of Rose of Sharon, planted
too closely to a chain-linked
fence, past all borders,
it beats still.

My mother tells me that she can't talk,
her hands are swollen
and I say that I am sorry
for the pinched nerve
that causes her pain,

my news, the connection I want
to make says, "I'll keep in touch."

I see in the grocery store,
on magazine racks, black
and white print. I see celebrities
and they say you are coming
for a second time. You will see
the heap that I speak
of and know the hearts again
that drove you home. I
tell you that they cry in their sleep
and take out the trash
on Monday.

II.

I imagine, sometimes
that you'll come to Denver first.
Your figure, your outstretched arms, sturdy
as a medal
will stop I-70 motorists. Twenty years ago
the lighted cross scared
me, the glare
from the mountain, shining
into my eyes
and down on a deep ascending road.

I learned to drive past accidents there
and how to make love in an apartment
above the Ace High Tap
to drink a case of beer between Golden
and Central City with Iowa friends,
we all knew that this was flight, the beginnings
of thinking that the soul
could be moved, uprooted,
and set down again,
the new ground replaced the past. There were new
skis for my birthday and unknown roommates
who drank shots and spoke of paying the "wooder" bill
the East was in the West.

I have looked for the place
without suffering.
Remembering resorts coins
of autumn aspen,
the history came back,
a grandmother
who stuffed baubles
in her chest of drawers, filling
them with a hundred losing sweepstakes tickets
a score of watches replacing
the one that her mother broke
on graduation day,

lonely records of dinners, dates,
the clothes were from her daughter's wedding
the father was too drunk
to walk down the aisle.

My mother made love to a black suit,
it wasn't blue
It was black shoes, tie
and trousers, the shoes were heavy
like concrete
and walked like jackhammers
across carpet, there was a pattern
on the toes
thick darkness to the heel.
It owned the utilities, the light switches
and newspapers rolled into fire
in my hearth home,
in my home hearth.
It was no banker, Diane.

That stalker, history. I married the son
of the superintendent of schools, a childhood prince
with manners and knew good people, people
who never crossed
a picket line or freed
a captive, goodness that render no justice

to the innocent caught
up in politics. Consensus
was not always kind. In practical living rooms,
looking for the place without pain,
the healers wore flat shoes
and chanted:
This house with its marble tile
and cherry finishes
will come down hard on disbelievers
and let me say no to Mrs. Waterbucket
when she calls to save the groundwater
or the groundswell
of public opinion on favored officials.
It will make my children Congressional scholars
and sweet music will flow from their fingers
and leave no smudges on my grand.
If I want I can hide my husband's mistress
in a walk-in
and he'll become the envy of every girl
who ever called a lawn care service.
His teeth will become orthodontically correct
and friends will imagine that he's big
on exotic vacations. This is my house. We built
it. It speaks for itself. It speaks foreign languages.
It speaks well.

III.

Lady Silence sits in leather interiors, driving past museums
and galleries. It is just as well. She cannot buy expression.

But once a musician played a flute below her hill
And she listened for a while, even walked down a slope.

His wild hair frightened her; he couldn't be taken out.
Still for a moment, he wished that he's stay in her world.

But such are dreams, and the best people have them. He
didn't stay. Before, he left Lady Silence took his instrument.

She keeps it in a firebox with crickets and sobs. All her
commitments are there, a last "I love you," dated somewhere
around 1962.

IV.

The air is absurd after music
so empty that three whistling birds
cannot fill the space. Pray for hot
tires and quick stops, the taxi door
slam, the hiss of wet streets
after rain when the pelting like
a heart beats, the night's pulse
from purple black clouds, unrelenting.

V.

Magnificent healer, most gentle of men, crimson leaf of new
birth, what horse-nosed
petal grows among thorns? I know that expression is Grace,
the word resounds, is heard
even in delicate whispers, the beauty rose, a once waxed
stem can thunder and split the sky.

Iris

Cut while in bloom,
you were an iris in middle pinks
and purples, mauve.
No one could see your fluid run
into the vase only
your soft petals, ornate fading
growing dark.

I watched you wither while
the world marveled at your hues.
How much more beautiful
could you become
until you became nothing swept
off the table until another spring?

The Raft

In my dreams
I am a swimmer stretched
out across the water
slightly bowed
a feather's spine
reaching for a raft
and I see you
and want to save
you and other people
as well. It is sad
that they were set adrift
on a wooden raft.
I reached for you
and the makeshift boat
pushed away teasingly
like in a love story
where things
don't work out
as planned; somebody
is left crying
wailing about fairness

and how sweetness
should reap the same.
I swam to you
pulled through the water
its transparent blue
and you moved
up to the very front
on the tilted board knowing
I couldn't catch
you like a high ball
in a summer dirt field
or a lucky fish
on its way back home
behind the rocks.
I don't know
if you laughed
because it is funny
how dreamers
imagine perfect endings
in deepest sleep.

Lucky Star

It is hard to tell
if the stars shine on me
locating breath
and I might be
in the right place
after wandering
between genres
and churches
doctrines and creeds.
I might be dressed
for the party
a welcomed guest
sweet and visited.
Roll from my fingers
hopeful passion
heaven's fine light
give me a home
in kind neighborhoods
under settled skies.

Fans

Ceiling fans turn
tiredly above our heads
time's movement
around years
the graying
the repose
of motion
after eyes
catch each blade
and stop
the circular dances
are exhausted still.

Mean Dog

A retriever stands
in the side street
repaired with tar
walking toward
a moving car.
It has seen meaner dogs
or known confinement
on a chain in the backyard
the pulling has made
it free. It is unafraid.
The car swerves
finally moves out
of the way. What nerve
to stand in front of steel
and pretend invincibility
we should be more like
that not quivering
when danger comes
to us in its varied forms.
Toughness is a virtue
in an uncertain world

where bombs go off
and fathers don't pay
support the body grows old
maybe the dog could not
see or hear
and there is something brave
about that as well.

Tourist

I hope that I'll never
be a tourist
and want to roam
ancient alleys
to cathedrals
ruby enshrined rooms
to read foreign menus
and drink local brew
a strong Christian wine
I will stay home
and complain about
the heat never finding
myself in a land
tediously unknown.
Moving drains and makes me long
for the past. I have spent
much time
in yesterday
where cities are kinder
and buildings
were beside the river

and a two-steeple
church could
be seen from the road
with orange cones
and reflecting barriers.
I have been places that
I should have never
left and so do not want
quaint cottages
or romantic rides
down celebrated streams.

Bright Air

Finally the open door

bright air

the bricks fall

the concrete exposes

bent steel rods

that have kept me

so unheard.

I have been yelling for decades

inside thick walls

Now I step out.

amazed at freedom

there is the unbelievable

the impossible

stacked straw

sweaty livestock

nature's mute feeling

inarticulate life

The outside knows me

My words are faint.

I remind them

and they recall the fetters, cut skin,

bruised bones
from trying to walk
on a straight path.
I am through the passage
my gait is steady
and shoes sound
one after another.
I move forward
without barricades
to be arriving at anticipated places
the lifted voice
talks announces sings
about confinement's end.

Backwards

Rabbits lucky
feet line the road
like they are waiting
for a parade.
The thing
that holds out
is the reason
why so many
creatures stand
in morning
slight water sitting
expecting
or content
with the new day.
When we wait
time goes
so slowly
that it might go
backwards
making its way
into the past.

Rabbits are
in grass behind
bushes tucked
into gardens
before they come
to see each other
in crooked rows
they must greet
and appreciate
their kind
and onlookers
are the ones that
think dreams
will materialize.

Exchange

The flowers aren't silk
but they are fake
like plastic fruit
with real flaws
the apples and oranges
the grapes
disapproving mothers
toward suitors
flattering words
but a false exchange
they fool visitors
confound them
which was not their
initial function.
I wanted beauty
arranged fiction
to last to stay in place
and never to change
the lilies with no smell
neither of freshness
no age. Their stems

are unbelievably straight
reach upward
at the room's center
to the right height
short people can see
across them talk
to each other
without leaning too much
and their petals
exist perfectly
in space. They
can never leave
or find the end
of their journey
across time. Yet
they do not cry
or fuss. They
are contained
in a gray vase
and can only stand
still being decoration.

Dietrich

Do you ever tire of the silence?
Does it move you to books?
The story of a man in prison
in dark uncertain times
with prayers for his release
letters are to his parents
and to dear friends who know
his fate better than grocery lists
or mundane common chores
Do you ever look down on poetry
for what it cannot achieve?
It cannot ride horses making
quick getaways from persecution.
It has no real agency
beyond the response
of the heart not beating cruel
regimes with verbs. I believe
in words, and that is my joy
and also my sorrow
attempting to make them stick
so others can move freely

so that the mind can open
a steel grinding movement
then liquid reaches the surface
there is promise again.
Cutting metal is an exact
art and requires the worker
to wear gloves in case of accidents.
I know there will be
misunderstanding
people who ignore insights
who dismiss knowledge
fancy lies to decipher
the man in prison shuns
fearfulness wanting bravery
more than pity. He is like us
in his imposed confinement
when captors are not kind
and real action is out. We
turn the pages to see what
happens to the chained hero
on paper, in another time.

Cloud Watch

I watched clouds,
played a child's
game saying what
they resembled until
high moisture
became the same
mass common concern
with no variation
and I wonder
if that is what it
is to grow old
acquainted with
the above
the heavens
where jets streak
and birds rise
from marshes
in a Southern
land near the sea.
The single figure
the only one

that might nourish
and give energy
but it cannot
be separated
cannot be its own
now when the car
drives fast down
the interstate
other cars passing
never knowing
how the prospect fails,
is limited
with the attempt
to name.

Loss

I think of losing you
and the world
does not seem right
or fair or just
or able to relax
after ten hour days
when the feet swell
and the waves
leave the center
of the ocean
they leave
all they've known
to come to shore
where swimmers
stroke the birds
peck at the sand
looking for morsels
and then dropping
one that the surf
steals with its force
the foam coming

and going
in front of a house
with a palm tree
near the drive. I
lament the passing
of time crying
a little more
at small thoughts.

Mattie McClane (Kristine A. Kaiser) records the artist's struggle for relevancy in a material world. Her poems reference the public and the private realms. She offers prayers for the people of New Orleans before Hurricane Katrina and scatters notes of current events throughout her poetry. At the same time, her poetry is strikingly private, honestly probing the anxieties of being a poetess in an era when poetry is a lost art.

McClane is a graduate of Augustana College, earning a B.A. in the Humanities. She holds an M.A. in English from the University of Louisville and an M.F.A. in Creative Writing from the University of North Carolina at Wilmington. She has studied under Alison Lurie and Sena Naslund as far as fiction and under Dennis Sampson in poetry.

McClane works as a columnist in the Piedmont region of North Carolina and has published political commentary regularly for several years. Mattie McClane is the author of *Night Ship: A Voyage of Discovery, Wen Wilson, and Unbuttoning Light: the Collected Short Stories of Mattie McClane. Now Time* is her first book of poetry.